The Home Office and The Remote Worker

Making the Home Office Work for You and Your Business

2nd Edition
Revised and Updated

By
Jonathan Cook

Disclaimer: This opinion report was prepared by Jonathan Cook. Neither Jonathan Cook nor any agency thereof, nor any of their employees, makes any warranty, express or implied, or assumes any legal liability or responsibility for the accuracy, completeness, or usefulness of any information, apparatus, product, or process disclosed, or represents that its use would not infringe privately owned rights. Reference herein to any specific commercial product, process, or service by trade name, trademark, manufacturer, or otherwise does not necessarily constitute or imply its endorsement recommendation, or favoring by Jonathan Cook or any agency thereof.

Text copyright © 2013 – 2017 Jonathan Cook

All Rights Reserved

No part of the original text, rendering or other original contents of this book may be reproduced, stored, or transmitted in any form or by any means now known or hereafter discovered, without the written permission of the author.

All images in this book are believed to be in the public domain or are licensed and attributed for use as noted.

Covers photo: Licensed by https://thoroughlyreviewed.com/ CC by 2.0

Visit the author's website for more information.
https://sites.google.com/site/jccookauthor/

Table of Contents

Table of Contents..3
Executive Summary..5
Introduction...7
What is a Home Office...8
Common Types of Home and Virtual Offices.....................12
   Pseudo-Virtual Office..12
   Semi-Virtual Office..14
   Full-Virtual Office..15
   Businesses that are Poor Candidates for the Home Office..............17
Advantages to the Home Office..18
   Lower Fixed Costs..18
   Reduced Commute Time..19
   Environmentally Friendly..20
   Staff Flexibility..21
   Higher Worker Satisfaction..21
   Possible Higher Productivity..22
   Child Care..22
   Global Reach...23
   Rich Talent Pool...24
Disadvantages to the Home Office.....................................25
   Management Loss of Control.......................................25
   Cost Shifting to Remote Workers.................................26
   Possibly Higher Technical and Technical Support Costs...............27
   Security...28
   Undermines Collaboration and Communication.........28
   Lower Worker Satisfaction..29
   Productivity Impacts..30
   Child Care...30
   Talent Misrepresentation/Difficult Interviewing..........30
Personalities..32
   Identify Personality Types..32
   Personality Types That May Have Trouble.................33
Tools..35
   Home Office Feature Set..35
   Keep It Simple..38
   Use Existing Providers...39

Network..41
  Accessing a Central Network:...41
  Personal Use...43
Execution — Practical Steps to Make It All Work...............44
  Plan...44
  Select Personnel..45
  Contract with Consequences...45
  Trial Run..46
  Implement...47
  Observe and Evaluate..47
  A Note on Video Conferencing...48
Long Term Considerations..50
  Stay on Top of Hardware, Software and Security Updates..........50
  Maintain and Enforce Home Worker Contracts............................51
  Immediately Remove Access for Terminated or Returning
  Employees..51
  Enjoy the Results..52
Conclusion...53

Executive Summary

In any business money is the bottom line. We may hate to admit it and we may do our best to avoid the reality that money is the fuel that powers and the grease that lubricates the wheels of business.

It was once overheard in a faith based, missions driven medical hospital the phrase: *No Money No Mission*. In this phrase was the stark realization that the mission depended upon the money that was generated by chargeable medical services.

In today's tech savvy businesses the potential benefits of home offices and remote workers to sales, to customer support, to worker satisfaction, and ultimately to the bottom line, cannot be overlooked.

But is it right for your business? Does a home office environment, even for just a portion of your business, make sense? The hype is out on the wires, but where do you find the answers based on real experience?

The Author has real experience in setting up, and

working as, remote resources in virtual environments. The Author has long term experience working in virtual settings.

This report can help you decide upon, and implement, a home office environment for your business.

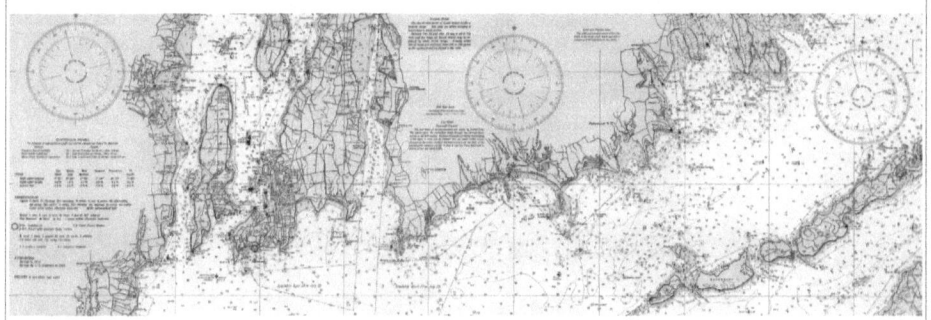

Introduction

Much has been said of the home office and its ability to save your company money as well as provide for more satisfied workers.

One report states that currently one in five workers around the world work remotely at least part of the time.[1]

However, little is written from the perspective of actual experience about how to really make it work.

This report will help you through the process of making a home office work.

This report is based on years of actual experience by the Author who has established and worked in a variety of remote and home office settings.

---

[1] http://www.reuters.com/article/2012/01/24/us-telecommuting-idUSTRE80N1IL20120124

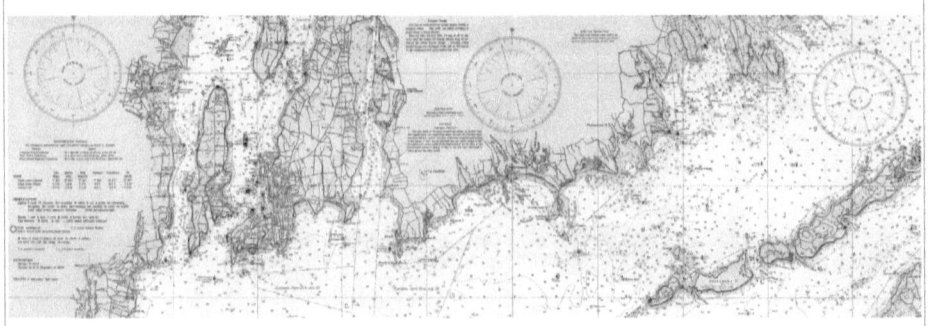

What is a Home Office

To be purely virtual is to be non-actual, or non physical. The concept of virtual reality is the act of modeling reality in a non-reality environment (generally in a computer).

So, in its purest sense, a home office is a virtual office and is, by definition, a non existent office (at least from the perspective of the business employer who does not maintain corporate office space for a home office worker).

This, of course, is not particularly practical in the real (and physical) world. People do exist and they need a place to work. As such the term virtual office is, in the opinion of the Author, a poorly defined concept.

Within the business world a common definition of the

virtual office is where a virtual office provider offers shared services and organized, professional physical office space for a (commonly) monthly or other periodic/per-use rental fee rather than a long term lease.

Most businesses that use a virtual office provider will use the rented space to interface with customers in a quality physical location with office services. This provides for a more professional and conventional interaction with the customer.

However, this falls short of the practical and the potential of the virtual office as well as the definition for a home office, and does not meet the requirements of the Author's definition for this report.

The Author chooses to define the home and virtual office (used interchangeably throughout much of this report) as a business work environment that does exist in the physical world as a physical place of conducted business. It is an office defined by the workers and the physical and communication connections required to make it function as a business.

This definition can run the gamut from a purely

networked office with no physical center/location (per the purist definition) to the traditional physical office in which the only virtual element is the workers who telecommute to the office from home, either temporarily (for example, during bad weather) or permanently.

A virtual office space provider is not a requirement of the virtual office definition, (but may be a practical element of the implementation for a business employing a purely virtual office as a business model) and a virtual office space provider, for all practical purposes, is not considered in a home office definition.

A home based office is, in essence, a virtual office that is located in the worker's home. The home office is used by a worker on a temporary or permanent basis to conduct work on behalf of an employer.

In general, a self employed person's home office is not considered a remote home office in this report as the home office is generally the main office of the business. However, a self employed person working out of their home may employ people who also work out of their homes. In this case, the concepts of a home office apply equally as well as to a larger corporation with main offices and home office workers.

Note however that this report provides a foundation that will work for all virtual and home office implementations. No matter what your virtual/home office needs, the base concepts are similar and can be implemented much the same way.

The Home Office...

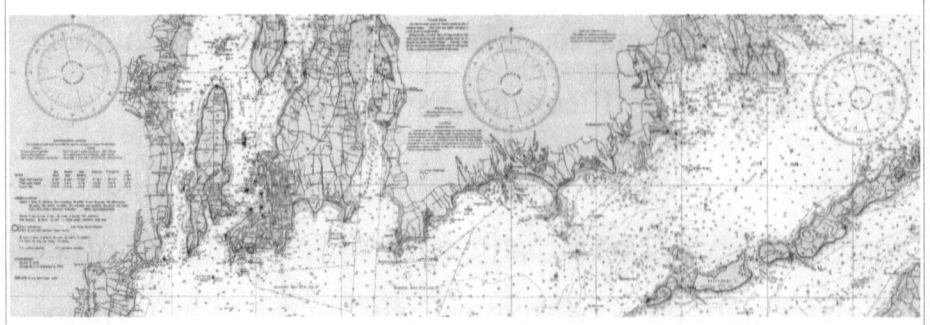

Common Types of Home and Virtual Offices

Pseudo-Virtual Office

As the name suggest this is a *fake* virtual office. That is not to say that the business is fake, simply that the implementation is a false virtual office in the sense of the

definition. A virtual office in this sense is simply a standard business office model of workers gathering in a common work location to conduct their business. The only virtual elements that may exist is that the workers, while temporarily off-site, can connect to the central office via remote access tools.

The most common application of the pseudo-virtual office is one in which workers access the central office after hours, when sick, or when away on business travel (and more often then not, away on vacation).

This environment generally benefits the owner/management structure of the business more than the remote workers.

Accessing the central office during business related travel is a practical use, but often results in long after hours work for the traveling staff.

Contagious ill workers accessing the central office remotely does have the practical effect of not infecting other office workers, but may interfere with the ill worker's recovery.

Non-travel, local access after hours simply means overtime work for the staff.

Semi-Virtual Office

This type of virtual office structure better fits the definition of a home office. The business may have a standard business office model or the virtual office provider model.

In either case the business will interface with customers at a professional office environment and the workers will have access to this professional office environment.

Image courtesy of David Castillo Dominici/FreeDigitalPhotos.net

In this situation the home worker is truly remote and maintains an ongoing fully functional home office from which all work is normally conducted. The only reason to travel to the central office is for traditional meetings with fellow workers or customers.

In the semi-virtual office the home workers can (and should be encouraged to) work a normal business day. However, the expectations of after hours, sick and long travel work hours may still creep into the work environment depending upon where on the scale of virtuality management views the work environment.

Full-Virtual Office

The full-virtual office truly fits the traditional definition of a virtual office. The full-virtual office has no central location. The only centralized aspect of the full-virtual office may be centralized servers housing business applications and data (even this can be decentralized or provided by an application/cloud provider).

The full-virtual office allows workers to be

located anywhere in the world and allows management to access the best talent and provide services across global time zones.

Since the full-virtual office has no central location, meetings and customer interface must be modified. The most common style of personal interaction is conducted using remote conferencing tools.

In the case of a localized full-virtual office the meetings are often conducted at the local coffee shop or hotel lobby (of which many are encouraging this practice as it promotes sales of their own products and services). Large meetings and conferences are conducted in rented conference space.

Like the other forms of virtual office, the expectations of after hours, sick and long travel work hours may still creep into the work environment. However, since the entire office is virtual the pressures to work unreasonable hours are often less as the management is also virtual.

In addition, for larger global virtual businesses the 24 hour nature of remote workers spanning multiple time zones lessens the pressure for workers in one time zone to put in unreasonable hours.

On the other hand, remote conference meetings that include far flung resources will require attendance at odd hours depending on the time zone difference.

Businesses that are Poor Candidates for the Home Office

Not all business models, or all departments within a business model, fit the paradigm of the home office.

Any business in which the workers must be on site at a central location does not fit the home office model. Common examples include manufacturing sites, retail sales locations, restaurants, etc.

These types of businesses require that people be on site to attend to the business needs. Until we have robots capable of performing to the same level as people, these business models will need real people on site.

However, management should review the business to see if any aspects can be virtualized to the advantage of the business. For example, a manufacturing site may need the assemblers on site, but designers and engineers can be off-site.

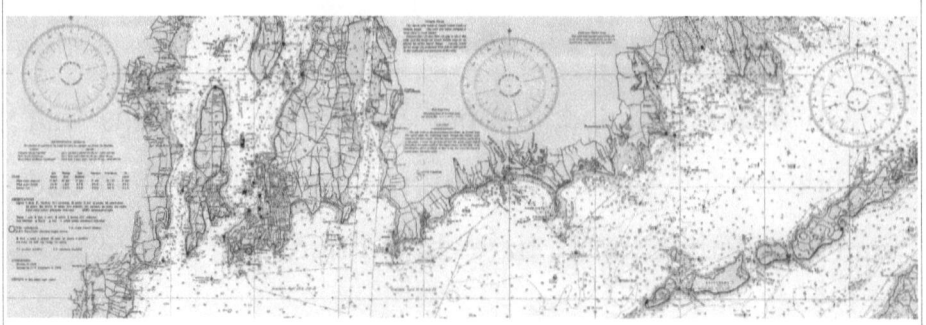

Advantages to the Home Office

The advantages of the home office have been documented in many publications, some more accurately than others.

This section will review the most common documented advantages as well as those actually experienced by the Author. It should be noted that not all advantages may apply to your specific business. In addition, be sure to review the disadvantages described in this report as they do exist.

Lower Fixed Costs

Depending on your implementation a key advantage to the home office is lower fixed costs for the business. This generally manifests in lower fixed office costs.

The Home Office...

If your business can function properly on fewer or no central office space resources, then that can result in a significant reduction in fixed expenses.

It should be noted that a certain percentage of the businesses fixed cost reduction is, in reality, a cost shifting to the remote worker. For example, less office space requires less heating/cooling.

However, your remote worker still requires heating and cooling at their location. Is the remote worker paying extra to heat and cool his/her home office to the advantage of the business? Cost shifting of this type should be recognized.

Reduced Commute Time

Any staff that telecommutes from home will no longer have to spend either the time or the money on commuting to the office. This results in less time on the road and possibly more time in the office.

However, management should not assume that reduced commute time automatically translates to more office work time. Management does not normally pay staff for the time and money spent on commuting.

In the same way management should not require or assume that the telecommuter will work the time that would otherwise be spent on commuting.

Environmentally Friendly

The Author considers this a weak argument for the home office. As mentioned, many of the real costs of office space and the subsequent environmental impacts are really just transferred to the worker and their home office expenses. In fact, most modern offices are probably more environmentally friendly (per capita space occupied) than the average home office.

It can certainly be argued that the reduced commute time for telecommute staff is environmentally significant, but the real business value is better measured in time, gas, and auto wear and tear.

However, if there is a business marketing advantage to the reduced environmental impacts then this can be advantageous.

Staff Flexibility

The Author does not recommend working staff overtime, but the need for overtime does, of course, occur.

The home office and a staff of telecommuters can provide increased flexibility in managing crunch times. A well connected home office can take advantage of varying time zones, reduced commute time and the home environment that allows a worker to be more comfortable while working late. However, management should not abuse this.

Higher Worker Satisfaction

This is a very common argument in favor of the home office and for most workers this higher satisfaction is true. However, management should observe both in-office and telecommute worker satisfaction closely.

Not everyone is happy with a home office. In-office staff may resent the perceived working advantages of the telecommuter and the telecommuter may not be satisfied with the team interactions and communications.

Every work environment varies so management should maintain open communications with the staff.

Possible Higher Productivity

Higher productivity is often touted as an advantage to the home office. However, higher productivity is not a guarantee.

A full day of work in a well connected home office is still just a full day of work. There may be some advantages to the reduced distractions of office chit-chat but this can be just as easily counteracted by the increased personal distractions of the home environment.

Management should not expect higher per hour productivity. Management should monitor productivity to be sure it is not reduced with a home office.

Child Care

The ability for workers to better manage their child care needs can be a key advantage to the home office. However, it is not a panacea for child care needs or productivity.

For example, a worker that telecommutes for the advantage of eliminating child care and keeping the child(ren) at home while they work will face innumerable distractions throughout the work day. As such, productivity may be an issue.

On the other hand this may be a key benefit to the worker and for management interested in retaining a valuable employee regardless of productivity impacts.

Image courtesy of digitalart/FreeDigitalPhotos.net

Management should consider all aspects of child care needs when considering the home office.

Global Reach

Well connected home offices, especially time diverse home offices spanning multiple time zones, can be effective in providing your business with a global reach.

Even without wide representation across time zones a home office can provide greater flexibility in managing global activities by allowing for greater worker flexibility and reduced costs.

This will not apply to every business model, but can be a great advantage to those models to which it can apply.

Rich Talent Pool

A home office offers a business the opportunity to recruit and retain workers from anywhere in the world. A well connected home office can manage staff located anywhere and can recruit staff with unique talents and location dependent advantages that would require the expenditure of greater resources for a physical office.

For example, a U.S. based business conducting business in France can be greatly advantaged with remote local staff that can fluently speak the language as well as manage contact (and even physical) facilities in country. In this situation, a physical based business might have a more difficult time implementing a remote office location to the same standards as their existing facilities.

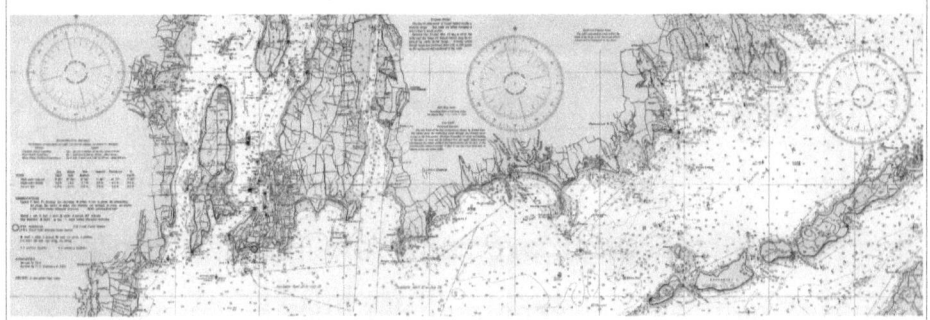

Disadvantages to the Home Office

Some of the disadvantages of the home office have already been suggested in the previous sections. However, they will be elaborated upon here.

Management Loss of Control

In general, management likes to see their staff in chairs, in the office, from which they can then observe and manage their staff. Management tends to be uncomfortable with remote workers as they appear to be out of touch and, frankly, are often forgotten by the managers.

This is more prevalent when a physical office is implementing new home office practices. Businesses that are formed as virtual offices may be able to avoid this tendency.

Established management in physical offices that are implementing home office practices may benefit from training to help them overcome the perceived loss of control, both as a psychological affect and a practical management effect.

Cost Shifting to Remote Workers

As mentioned, much of the savings that the home office concept claims to achieve is really just cost shifting to the employee. In many situations the employee takes over the costs of internet connections, phone lines, heating, cooling, facility maintenance (who pays for a clogged toilet during working hours?), etc.

As such, cost savings is really cost shifting. This is not to say that cost savings are not real. Cost shifting to a home office may be less expensive than the corresponding costs of a cubical in a physical office.

Management and the remote home staff need to recognize these advantages and disadvantages and be open and honest about who covers what costs (as well as any legal and tax implications).

Possibly Higher Technical and Technical Support Costs

Depending on your business model, technical requirements, and virtual cost structure, a home office may have a higher per person technical cost than a physical office.

Image courtesy of cooldesign/FreeDigitalPhotos.net

For example, each home worker will likely require one or more workstations, laptops, tablets, mobile phones, etc. and may require separate firewalls, security software, VPN connections, software licenses, etc.

In addition, unless each worker is well versed (and authorized) in maintaining this remote infrastructure the costs of this maintenance may be higher for a home office.

There may be other, less technical, support costs as well. Who supplies (and pays for) pencils and paper, training materials, mobile phone plans, general office equipment, etc.

All of these need to be considered for a successful home office.

Security

In today's home office security is a prime consideration. This report is not designed to be a security primer, but security must be considered.

As mentioned this can increase support costs and without a centralized security plan a home office can end up with a disparate jumble of security implementations.

Undermines Collaboration and Communication

A home office can undermine the communication and collaboration common in centralized physical offices.

The Author has observed directly and through

research that not all remote staff handle the lack of personal interaction well.

With a well connected home office and a motivated staff this can be overcome. However, it should not be ignored by management.

Lower Worker Satisfaction

As much as the media and management consultants talk up the increased worker satisfaction found in the

home office, it is not universal. Not everyone likes the home office concept.

This dissatisfaction is generally reported and observed to revolve around lack of the personal interaction as found in a centralized physical office. In addition, other issues can also arise.

Management needs to be open to any criticisms from staff and to be alert to worker dissatisfaction.

Productivity Impacts

Similar to satisfaction, productivity improvements are not guaranteed. As mentioned above, management needs to be tuned into productivity and consider the impacts or benefits of the home office on productivity.

Child Care

Please see Child Care in *Advantages to the Home Office*.

Talent Misrepresentation/Difficult Interviewing

The Author's experience and research indicates that talent is a poorly addressed issue in both the virtual and physical office environments.

The search for talent is an ongoing process for many businesses and, with the advent of advanced communication technologies, the search and the interview of prospects are often done online and/or over the phone with candidates in far off locations.

The Author has conducted many remote/phone interviews of candidates and a surprising number of candidates clearly misrepresented themselves on their resumes and in their interviews.

One of the most common tactics observed was using an internet search for answers to interview questions during the actual interview. Over the phone the candidate could be heard rapidly typing on the keyboard immediately after the question, then obviously reading a technical article or sales pitch back to the interviewer.

Not every interviewer is observant to this and the other tactics that candidates may use to misrepresent themselves. The Author's interview experience indicates that these tactics are more prevalent amongst candidates seeking contract positions as opposed to those seeking permanent employment.

The Author recommends that candidates be interviewed in person whenever possible and that special care should be taken when searching and interviewing candidates remotely.

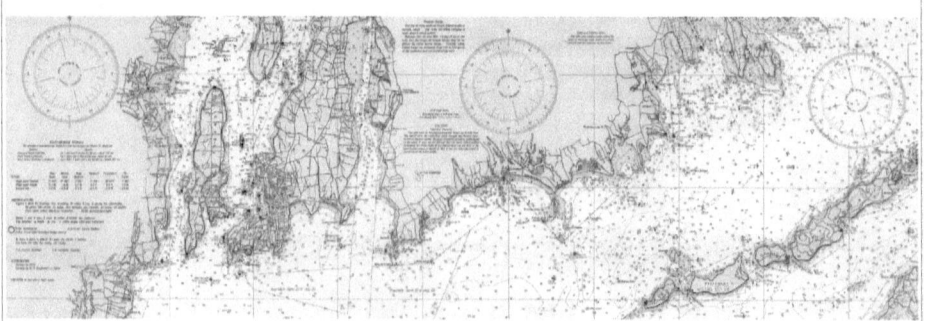

Personalities

While this report is not designed to be a psychological analysis of personality types, it can be helpful to consider basic personality concepts and traits when evaluating the move to a home office environment.

Identify Personality Types

It can be constructive to consider the personalities of those individuals under consideration for remote work. In an established centralized physical office that is considering implementing a home office, there will likely be existing staff under consideration to make the move to remote work.

You should review carefully the appropriateness of both the job profile and the personality profile of the worker up for consideration.

In a new business start-up that is going to form as a virtual office you will need to discern new candidates at the time of the interviews and offers.

Either way you will want to be assured that the staff is appropriate for a virtual/home office environment.

Personality Types That May Have Trouble

There are a few personality types that may not be as effective in a home office as in a physical office.

People who are very conversational and thrive on direct face-to-face communications may not do well. On the other hand these people may actively seek contact over the wire and actually be quite effective.

People who are less tech-savvy may need additional tech training to perform confidently in a home environment.

People who do not do well under pressure. Since they will be isolated and will not have direct interaction with supporting team members the remote home office person needs to be resilient.

People with poor phone skills.

People who need structure and well defined time boundaries.

People who need ongoing management interaction.

People with poor organizational skills.

Complainers and those who lack a positive attitude.

You can further your research on virtual/home office personality types by checking out these links:

https://www.bloomberg.com/news/articles/2009-06-16/is-there-a-virtual-worker-personality-businessweek-business-news-stock-market-and-financial-advice

http://gigaom.com/2011/08/03/top-5-personality-traits-of-successful-web-workers/

http://en.wikipedia.org/wiki/Telecommuting

The Home Office...

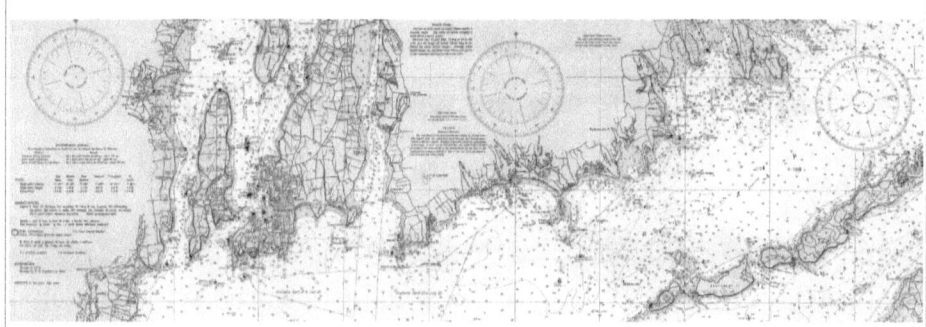

Tools

The tools that you might use to implement your home office environment can vary to the same degree as any other office process. However, the key to selecting a particular tool is not in the tool itself, but in the security and ease of use. This report will not recommend a particular tool, but will assess what to look for in a tool.

Home Office Feature Set

In order to implement a basic home office you need to provide for remote access. In often used jargon, the remote office must be set up to support the *telecommuter*.

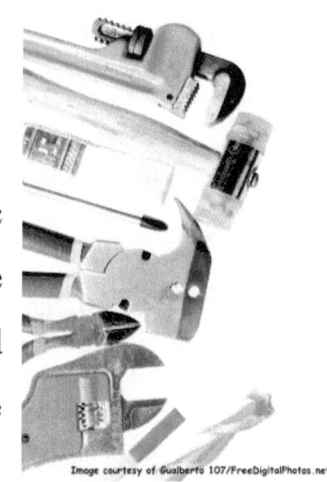

The Home Office...

Will the telecommuter be in a physical office (regularly or at all), at a remote satellite location, or in a home office? Will the telecommuter be on the road with a laptop or tablet or just a smart phone? Regardless the remote worker will need some basic features with which to conduct work.

The work to be conducted will also impact the feature set. Reading and responding to emails requires a different level of complexity than an engineer working with advanced tools.

In all cases the remote user will need at least:

Some type of workstation. Generally a laptop, tablet, phone or some combination of these.

Virus and other security software local to the workstation. This is also important on tablets and phones.

Workstation networking capability. The most secure networking is via a hard wire connection (i.e. an internet service provider) using a secure Virtual Private Network (VPN) connection.

In a mobile situation private wireless networks and phone service data wireless (as provided by a wireless service provider) is less secure but can be secure enough for most business.

The least secure is free network wireless as provided by coffee shops, restaurants and other public locations. Although there are security solutions for these, it is recommended that this type of networking never be used.

Access to central storage and/or apps. Most businesses require some type of central data and application repository and access to this repository.

This is usually accomplished with a networking simulator that makes the central site available to the remote user as an extension to the workstation environment.

This can be as simple as the built in tools found in most operating systems, or add-ons that provide their own private security and networking features.

Phone services. This is usually handled by standard phones or cell phones. In addition you can explore third party tools that provide phone services over the network and the Internet (Voice over Internet Protocol or VoIP). Depending on your needs these can be feature rich and low cost.

Conference services. This is a broad requirement that can be met a number of ways.

Simple conferencing can be accomplished with a phone system's conference feature. More complex voice and video conferencing can be accomplished with online or private conferencing tools via your private network and the internet.

The conferencing concept is one that you can start simple and build up as needed.

Security. In all cases of setting up a home office you should be especially aware of security. You must be sure that all aspects of your home office are secure at every point of use and connection.

Keep It Simple

One concept regularly overlooked is to keep the home office simple. Many businesses in their quest to improve efficiency and productivity will often load up on tools, applications and features in the vain belief that more is better.

In fact the opposite is usually true. It is better to use a few good tools well than to use many tools poorly.

In addition, be wary of automatically loading too many background applications onto a workstation, tablet, phone or other device. This is a particularly prevalent problem in larger organizations with centralized security and system maintenance departments that can, quite frankly, act as dictators over worker's systems.

These centralized departments can often load too many items onto a device, slowing performance to a crawl, rendering it useless to the worker.

Use Existing Providers

Along the line of *Keep it Simple* is to avoid re-inventing the wheel. In other words, where possible, use existing software and providers to accomplish your home office needs.

Your business model will help you determine this requirement. Some highly specialized business models may require custom software to meet their home office needs. Other models will do just fine with basic and inexpensive off-the-shelf tools.

Most specialized business software designed to use a local network to access remote data (client-server model) will likely work fine accessing data remotely over the internet if the connectivity mimics a local network.

Browser based software is generally already internet and remote aware and will also work well. You will need to assess your unique requirements but in all cases validate that the security is appropriate.

The Home Office...

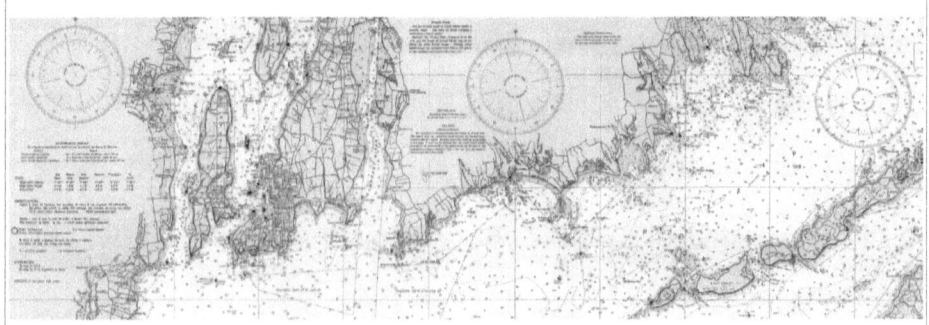

Network

Possibly the most critical element of a home office is the network. Do not skimp on network performance. Even the fastest workstation will slow to a crawl if the network behind it is slow.

There are a number of ways to create a home office network using the internet as well as a number of internet providers. Logic dictates that you find the fastest performance for the least cost and with proper security.

This will likely vary by region and local conditions. As such you may need to review a number of providers and setups to get the best results in a specific location.

Accessing a Central Network:

The remote worker's need to access the internet is

The Home Office...

generally straight forward and can be handled with off-the-shelf small office/home office (SOHO) tools. However, connecting into a central site may be more complex. Security is paramount. You must be sure that hackers cannot breach your security.

There is a variety of hardware and software to manage this, but a central theme should be the security of the log-on process.

Each worker should have a unique, strong user-id and password combination (there are also deeper log-on processes that employ such things as security questions, clock tokens and pictures).

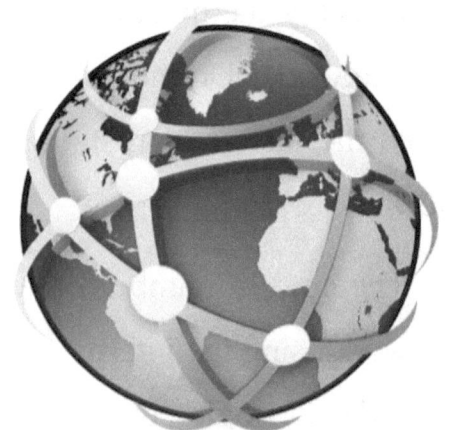

It is recommended that you employ some type of rotating authentication token where the user enters their own personal password in combination with the numbers/letters on the personally possessed token device.

The token updates its own display periodically such

that the user always has a changing strong password.

Personal Use

Be aware that workers (and especially remote workers) will likely use the tools and network for their personal use. This may or may not impact productivity.

Many argue that personal use takes time away from productive work for which the worker is paid. Others argue that personal breaks from the monotony of work actually improves productivity.

Management will need to determine how to handle this. The Author's experience indicates that among professionals this is not a productivity problem but only you can determine this for your unique situation.

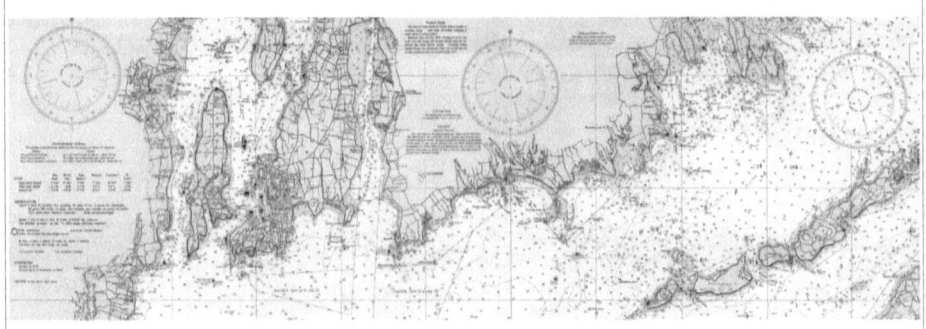

Execution — Practical Steps to Make It All Work

You have made the decision to implement a home office. Now what?

Plan

Planning for the home office sounds obvious but is often not done at all or done poorly. Obviously each situation is unique and will require unique levels of planning. The following will help.

Make final decisions on personnel, network equipment and processes.

Finalize providers.

Determine security protocols.

Finalize and license workstation tools.

Establish installation and maintenance protocols.

Select Personnel

Established businesses will likely need to select personnel to participate in the new home office implementation. Allow your research to guide you in this process. Of course, be sure that anyone you select actually wants to work remotely.

New businesses (or businesses expanding using virtual office processes) will integrate the selection process into the interview and hiring process.

Once selected it is recommended that you begin the transition quickly as most workers will want to implement the changes rapidly.

Contract with Consequences

You may wish to implement your home office using remote worker contracts that stipulate the rules of remote work. The contents of the contracts are up to management but should include rules to insure security as well as provide for real consequences should the rules be violated.

Image courtesy of digitalart/FreeDigitalPhotos.net

You may wish to consider monitoring software, if not already in place, to insure that the contract is being followed. Of course, follow all applicable laws regarding monitoring. It is recommended that workers be fully informed of any monitoring.

Trial Run

Management may wish to implement a trial run of the home office prior to a complete implementation. This is more applicable to established businesses with existing physical offices.

New businesses or existing businesses expanding with virtual offices may not benefit extensively from a trial run as the virtual office should already be a de facto part of the development plan.

The Home Office...

Implement

Now it is time to implement. If you have already established a trial run and it is going well the implementation may be as simple as a memo stating the trial is over and the home office is now established.

Otherwise, verify that all of the hardware, software, protocols, documentation, support and contracts are in place; that everything is working; and that management and the home workers are satisfied with the situation. If everything looks OK, then turn on the home office.

Observe and Evaluate

With remote workers out of sight it is easy to put them out of mind as well. Be careful. Do not forget the home worker. Even if they are performing as expected and communicating as needed, be sure not to forget their contributions. Manage them as you would any worker.

With this in mind, be sure to observe your home office and validate that it is working and meeting the expectations planned for it. While this should not be dictatorial in action, you should be able to evaluate that the home office is working.

This evaluation may be as simple as the standard company employee evaluation process or as complex as evaluating metrics gathered from monitoring tools. However you determine the results, be sure the home office meets expectations otherwise it may not be viable in the long run.

In evaluating the home office be sure to consider the hard to measure *worker satisfaction*. If workers are happy, even if results are only *good enough,* the home office may still be a success as worker satisfaction should be a priority of business.

A Note on Video Conferencing

Video conferencing is a powerful meeting tool and in today's technical world a big cost saver compared to office/conference space and travel expenses.

However, there is the temptation to view video conference meetings (and home offices in general) as a casual, lowbrow form of meeting.

In the home office and in video conferencing you

should demand of staff not only the same performance as expected in any office environment but also the same grooming and presentation standards.

Image courtesy of Renjith Krishnan/FreeDigitalPhotos.net

These standards can vary greatly, of course, and it is not for the Author to dictate any particular standard. However, in the Author's observations the virtual office and video conferencing can be less effective if established standards are not maintained.

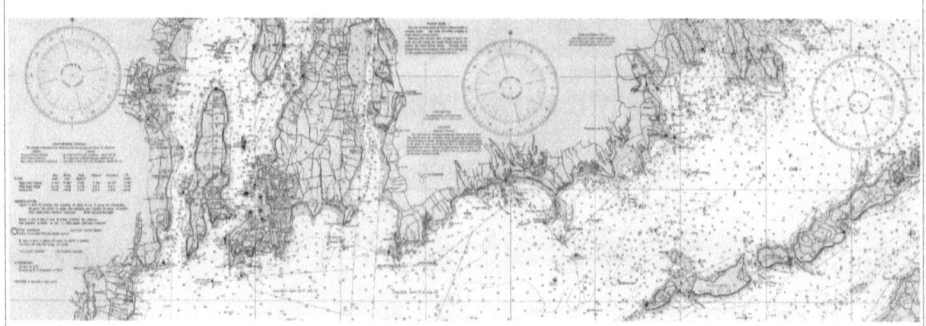

Long Term Considerations

Now that the home office is up and running there are some long term consideration to manage.

Stay on Top of Hardware, Software and Security Updates.

It should be needless to say, but be sure and keep up on the various updates and upgrades to be sure that your home office is as up-to-date as any physical office.

This is easily managed in a physical office in which all workers are co-located. However, it is very easy to overlook when your office is remote.

Remote management software with *push* tools can be useful. These tools will push changes to a remote computer insuring that updates are completed on a remote site. It is recommended that remote workers be aware of changes before and as they take place. Otherwise the failure of a change that causes a dead workstation can be an unexpected surprise.

In addition, as pointed out before, do not overload workstations with to much software as it may slow systems to a crawl and make work impossible.

Maintain and Enforce Home Worker Contracts

If home worker contracts are in place be sure to maintain them, remind workers of them and, if necessary, enforce them.

Immediately Remove Access for Terminated or Returning Employees

With security and contract enforcement in mind you should have a policy and process in place to immediately remove remote access for any worker that has lost the privilege of remote access.

This could be due to termination or a home worker permanently returning to the physical office. Regardless, it is a security risk to provide remote access to anyone not authorized.

Enjoy the Results

As a final word. If all goes well, then enjoy the results!

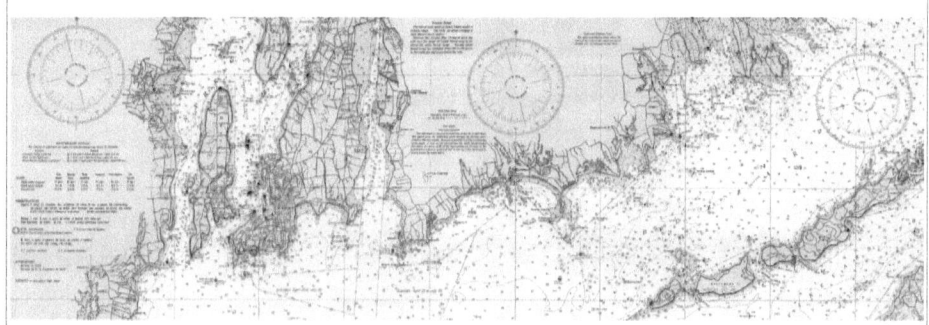

Conclusion

This report has provided the reader with the opinion of the Author based on decades of experience in the field of Information Technology.

It provides insights and advice that in the opinion of the Author will help you fine tune your home office and remote access implementations by introducing elements and ideas often overlooked in the standard professional texts and consulting services.

After reading this text it is hoped that you will be able to find new ways to enhance your business techniques and improve your results.

www.ingramcontent.com/pod-product-compliance
Lightning Source LLC
Chambersburg PA
CBHW021044180526
45163CB00005B/2280